COLORING BOOK·FOR

FLOWER LOVERS

By: Sylvie Cyr

ARCHWAY
PUBLISHING

Archway Publishing books may be ordered through booksellers or by contacting:

Archway Publishing
1663 Liberty Drive
Bloomington, IN 47403
www.archwaypublishing.com
1 (888) 242-5904

ISBN: 978-1-4808-5288-4 (sc)
ISBN: 978-1-4808-5289-1 (e)

Print information available on the last page.

Archway Publishing rev. date: 02/16/2018

I Love you

LACe

Printed in the United States
By Bookmasters